What can I do?

Written by Keith Gaines

Illustrated by Tony Kenyon

Nelson

Pat the pig sat in his house.

"What can I do?"
said Pat the pig.

"I will go and see Meg the hen."

"Hello, Meg,"
said Pat the pig.
"What can I do?"

"Can you help me to paint?"
said Meg.
"I am painting
the front of my house."

"Yes, I will help you to paint," said Pat the pig.

They painted all over the front of Meg's house.

"Thank you, Pat,"
said Meg.

"I will go and see Jip the cat," said Pat the pig.

"Hello, Jip,"
said Pat.
"What can I do?"

"Can you help me to fish?"
said Jip.

"Yes, I will help you to fish," said Pat.

They got lots of fish from the river.

"Thank you, Pat,"
said Jip.

"I will go and see Sam the fox," said Pat the pig.

"Hello, Sam,"
said Pat.
"What can I do?"

"Can you help me
to make some jam tarts?"
said Sam.

"Yes, I will help you
to make some jam tarts,"
said Pat.

They filled the tarts with jam.

"Can you help me
to eat the jam tarts?"
said Sam.

"Yes, I will,"
said Pat the pig.

They ate the jam tarts.
Yum, yum.

"Thank you, Sam,"
said Pat.